The University of Birmingham

School of Government and Society

International Development Department

The British Gurkhas After Resettlement
How They Can Successfully Contribute Towards Nepal's Development From The UK

Submitted: 20th July 2012

By: Anna Townsend

Programme of Study: Master of Science in Poverty Reduction and Development Management

ACKNOWLEDGEMENTS

I am grateful to Jeremy Lefroy MP for taking such an interest in the Gurkhas in his Stafford constituency and for encouraging me to research and write this dissertation; I truly hope that it is useful.

Huge thanks go to the Queens Gurkha Signals at Beacon Barracks, Stafford who have made me so welcome and have shared their hopes, dreams and concerns for Nepal; it has been a privilege to hear them. Particular thanks go to Capt Teshar Gurung who arranged the meetings and wisely contributed, SSgt Jaya Prakash who escorted me around camp and looked after all my needs and Lt Col Ronnie Westerman who provided wonderful hospitality; I hope we shall remain friends.

In Aldershot I wish to thank Major Khimprasad Gauchan for his time and thoughts, as ever he was wise and considerate. Lastly I must thank my husband Simon who has allowed me to become involved in the wonderful lives of the Gurkhas and gave me such a great gift when I accompanied him to live in Nepal several years ago.

CONTENTS

ABSTRACT

The number of Nepalis choosing to migrate from Nepal to live and work abroad is growing and it is estimated that 20 to 29% of Nepal's GDP is remittance income (Migration Information Source). There is little intention, articulated in Nepal's Poverty Reduction Strategy Paper, to constructively manage migration and no mention of how to facilitate a positive contribution from its Diaspora population (Government of Nepal, 2007).

Many Nepalis have settled in the UK following service in the Gurkha regiments of the British Army. In 2009 their post-service terms and conditions were altered so that they and their immediate families could have indefinite leave to remain in the UK for the rest of their lives (UK Border Agency). This change has been negative for Nepal as a whole; the economy receives less remittance income from Gurkha soldiers who now invest in their future in Britain and the country has lost out on well educated family members who in the past returned to Nepal to work and establish businesses. As a further example, vulnerable women supported by my own charity, Women Without Roofs – Nepal, who were employed to do domestic work for ex-Gurkhas, have lost their jobs.

This paper seeks to understand how Nepal could put in place policies to make the most of its Diaspora population, and what these communities could do to contribute to Nepal's development. There is both a need to exploit the positive aspect of its Diaspora, namely their income and skills, and to protect against the negative effects. What can be learnt from other countries about successful management of migrants and Diasporas?

In particular the research will consider the case of serving and retired Gurkhas, and their wives that now live in the UK. It will examine how they could specifically contribute to Nepal's development and through quantitative and qualitative research allow them to suggest ways to aid Nepal.

PART ONE: INTRODUCTION

1.1 RESEARCH CONTEXT AND PROBLEM STATEMENT

Nepal is the second poorest country in Asia and ranked 157th in the UN's Human Development rankings for 2011 (UNDP, 2011). The Government of Nepal, in its first Poverty Reduction Strategy Paper, acknowledged that "poverty in Nepal has persisted for decades, and it is recognised as a deep-seated and complex phenomenon, for which there are no quick and easy solutions" (Government of Nepal, 2003, p1). Both physical and economic infrastructures are weak or absent and there are limited employment opportunities. Where development initiatives have been successful, they have proved difficult to sustain. Ongoing political unrest and calls for reform in the last two decades by the Maoist party have also increased insecurity and undermined the existing limited social structures (European External Action Service, 2010).

Nepal is also disadvantaged by its geography; being landlocked and mountainous has contributed to its economic and social isolation. Trade between Nepal and its two neighbours, India and China, has been hindered for centuries due to a lack of navigable rivers and year-round weather proof roads. Transport costs for goods and people remain exorbitant and economists have long been aware of the link between these costs and slow economic development (Sachs, 2005). Another longstanding problem is the role that the Hindu caste system plays in holding back development and caste often manifests as deep rooted inequality and prejudice (Government of Nepal, 2003).

It is from this background then that the British Army recruits Nepali men to serve in its regiments. The soldiers have historically been recruited from the rural and hilly Gorkha district of Nepal and have come to be known as Gurkhas, though they may be from any district. A peace treaty signed in 1816 permitted Gurkhas to volunteer for service in the East India company's Army and a modified version of the agreement continues today, though the number of Gurkhas recruited has steadily reduced and today stands at just 200 per annum (British Army, 2012).

Following high profile campaigns in 2007 and 2009 the British Government conceded to allow all Gurkha soldiers and their immediate families to settle in the UK after their retirement; this is called 'indefinite leave to remain' and is not British citizenship. Provided they have served at least four years in the British Army they may settle in the UK and need not return to settle in Nepal as they were previously required to do so (UK Border Agency). Between May 2009 and September 2011 a total of 7025 settlement visas were issued to former Gurkhas and their wives by the Home Office, this figure does not include children (Green, 2012).

The decision to allow Gurkhas to remain in Britain has been celebrated by their supporters, yet the impact of the decision on the rest of Nepal has been largely overlooked. Gurkhas now look towards their future in the UK and therefore no longer send large amounts of money home to Nepal to be invested and spent there. Towns such as Dharan that previously received large numbers of retired Gurkhas flourished as a result of their planning and entrepreneurial skills and were not only orderly but also booming economically. Council services, such as rubbish collections, were introduced and the entire town population benefited (Blakely, 2011). In short, Nepal has lost a valuable resource now that the Gurkhas do not return to Nepal and consequently its development has been negatively impacted.

Diaspora groups, of which the Gurkhas are one example, can be regarded as 'communities of practice' (Page & Mercer, 2012). There are countless potential positive effects of their remittance behaviour, not only in the transmission of money but also social ideas and values. Given that as a group they are in the process of settling in Britain and assuming a new Diaspora way of life, now is a perfect time to 'contribute to the challenge of establishing and institutionalising more progressive equitable lifestyles' with the aim of furthering development in Nepal (p15).

1.2 RESEARCH OBJECTIVES

This paper therefore seeks to generate a set of possible in ways in which the Gurkhas, under their new terms and conditions, can continue to assist in Nepal's development from the UK. It will search for not only economic measures but also social and political means of development that could be implemented by them or in which they could meaningfully participate.

Given that this paper's audience includes a member of the All-Party Parliamentary Britain-Nepal Group and action may be taken to facilitate the implementation of these development ideas the focus is on practical action. This paper will also attempt to suggest some responsibility for each of the ideas and next steps will be indicated. In doing so, it will focus on three main actors; the Gurkhas themselves, the British Government and the Nepali Government.

This paper does not 'take for granted the fact that remitting is intrinsic to a Diaspora lifestyle' and neither does it believe that all Gurkhas should be compelled to help Nepal develop (Page & Mercer, 2012). However it does assume that many Gurkhas want to make a meaningful contribution to Nepal and that the British Government has a moral obligation to help them given that Nepal has been disadvantaged now that the Gurkhas are settling in Britain rather than in Nepal. Of course the Nepali government is morally obliged to act in the interest of its citizens though, as will be discovered, may not be doing all it can.

1.3 BROAD METHODOLOGICAL AND ANALYTICAL APPROACH

The research approach is inductive and the aim has been to build development theory by casting a wide net and seeking for ideas and solutions to the problem stated above. During the literature review four main subject areas have been drawn upon; these are 1) The nature of migration from Nepal, 2) The effect of migration on home countries, 3) Diasporas and how best to harness them and 4) Policies to maximise the development benefits of Diasporas.

First hand research has also been utilised and serving Gurkhas and their wives from Stafford and Aldershot have been invited to suggest ways to help Nepal themselves; by participating in this process it has empowered them and generated ownership for the ideas. This is a springboard to further action once the dissertation writing process has finished. Gurkhas' attitudes towards and their potential ability to participate in the ideas generated by the desk-based research has also been gathered through focus groups and one-to-one interviews.

Mr Mahesh Bhattarai, an Executive Director of Nepal Rastra Bank in Kathmandu was also interviewed to find out more about Nepal's Diaspora bonds and the country's general intentions towards migrants.

1.4 STRUCTURE OF THE PAPER

Part Two provides an overview of current literature pertaining to Diaspora groups and communities and in particular gives the views of the World Bank towards their role in development which at this time is particularly favourable.

Part Three, the main body of the paper, catalogues all of the ideas generated by the literature review and introduces initiatives suggested by the Gurkhas themselves. Each idea is analysed for the possible contribution it could make to development, what the Gurkhas themselves think about the proposal and who needs to take action to implement it.

In Part Four the ideas are summarised and recommendations for action are given.

The conclusion in Part Five considers further the moral rationale for involving the Gurkha Diaspora in Nepal's development and cautions against adding to the pressure on them to contribute financially.

PART TWO: LITERATURE REVIEW

2.1 THE NATURE OF MIGRATION FROM NEPAL

The migration of large groups of people from one region to another has been long been observed and commented upon. As transport systems have evolved people movement has become easier and migration patterns have been affected. Initially migration was limited to a national phenomenon, usually from rural to urban areas; following that the movement of peoples between countries became more commonplace leading to the circumstances today where great numbers of people migrate between continents. Of course, these migration patterns are not mutually exclusive and occur concurrently. Castles and Miller (1998) provide an overview of the history of migration from the seventeenth century and highlight four major events, these being; colonial migration and the slave trade, migration due to industrialisation between 1850 and 1920, the effects of the Second World War and the globalisation of migration following the war. Hatton and Williamson (1998) also write about the great movement of people from Europe to the New World during the latter part of the 19th century.

Most pertinent to the subject of this paper is the history of migration from Asia provided by Castles and Miller (1998). This region is home to large populations and characterised by surplus manpower; as a result the area has long been seen as a source of inexpensive labour. The cheap labour force was first exploited by colonial rulers in India, including, though not exclusively, the British. During the time of colonial rule in India, Nepal was isolated and did not participate in the nascent global market for goods and people. However, during the 1970s and 1980s international migration from Asia grew dramatically and Nepal featured in this change by sending large numbers of workers to the Gulf region which was experiencing rapid economic growth.

Gurkha recruitment and the resultant form of medium-term migration of Gurkhas to Hong Kong and India prior to the 1960s were exceptional people movements, rather than a part of the general pattern of out-migration from Nepal that exists today (Castles & Miller, 1998). Massey, Axinn and Ghimire (2010), in reference to Nepal, state that 'population mobility remained at a virtual standstill for more than a century, both internally and internationally'. In The Economist (2009) an insightful article describes how Lahures, the derogatory Nepali name for the Gurkhas, has been adopted as the label for all Nepali migrant workers abroad today. This is simply because they were the first group to work overseas and no other name existed.

Three theories of migration, in the chronolgical order in which they were conceived, are also put forward by Castles and Miller (1998) to reason for and describe patterns of people movement. First neo-classical economic equilibrium theory attempted to explain the push-pull factor of migration and emphasised an individual's decision to migrate in order to maximise their utility and therefore income. This theory is viewed as overly simplistic because it ignores all non-economic factors; instead the historical-structural approach usurped it that places an emphasis on government policies to mobilise cheap labour. In particular this theory stresses the exploitation of poor countries by richer ones and the dependency of the former on the latter. Today, neither of these theories is much subscribed to, rather migration systems theory is the predominant paradigm which takes a holistic and far more nuanced view of the causes of migration.

Certainly Gurkhas do apply to the British Army to escape poverty and increase their earnings; yet important causes are overlooked if neo-classical economic equilibrium theory is used to explain their recruitment. The decision to migrate is seldom made by an individual on his own; instead it is most often a familial decision that takes into account the opinions of others. The historical-structural approach is similarly overly simplistic as Gurkhas willingly offer themselves for recruitment and compete for places; they are not conscripted into the British army. Migration systems theory is therefore a better attempt to understand the migration process and underscores the reciprocal links between Britain and Nepal. It allows the role of international relations to be recognised as well as the social networks between the Gurkhas themselves and the micro-structures they put in place to support each other. These not only aid and abet recruitment, but are utilised to help each other to settle into life in the Army and the UK more generally.

Though the number of Gurkha soldiers recruited from Nepal has dropped, the overall number of migrants leaving Nepal has risen as illustrated in figure 1 (Government of Nepal, 2010). More recently the outflow of people from the rural and hilly districts of Nepal has been attributed to environmental change and the associated drop in productivity of agricultural land that contributes to poverty (Massey, Axinn and Ghimire, 2010). Political violence and insecurity too have been blamed and the 'environment-security nexus' defined by Lee (2001, cited in Massey et al, 2010) has created new levels of misery. Certainly poverty is a key push factor for those leaving Nepal seeking work abroad and it has been examined in great detail at household level by Lokshin, Bontch-Osmolovski and Glinskaya (2010). They conclude 'that one-fifth of the poverty reduction in Nepal occurring between 1995 and 2004 can be attributed to higher levels of work-related migration and remittances sent home' (p323). The percentage of households receiving remittance income in 2004 was 32% and came at the end of a decade that had seen this proportion steadily rise. Not only had the number of households in receipt of remittances increased, but their value and percentage contribution to mean household expenditure had also risen to 44%. Therefore, over the period, Nepal had become far more dependent on remittances and this is most noticeable in rural areas indicating that a lack of rural job opportunities and low agricultural productivity were driving forces in prompting Nepali workers to seek employment overseas.

Figure 1: The net total of migrants during each five year period, that is, the total number of immigrants less the annual number of emigrants, including both citizens and noncitizens. Data are five-year estimates.

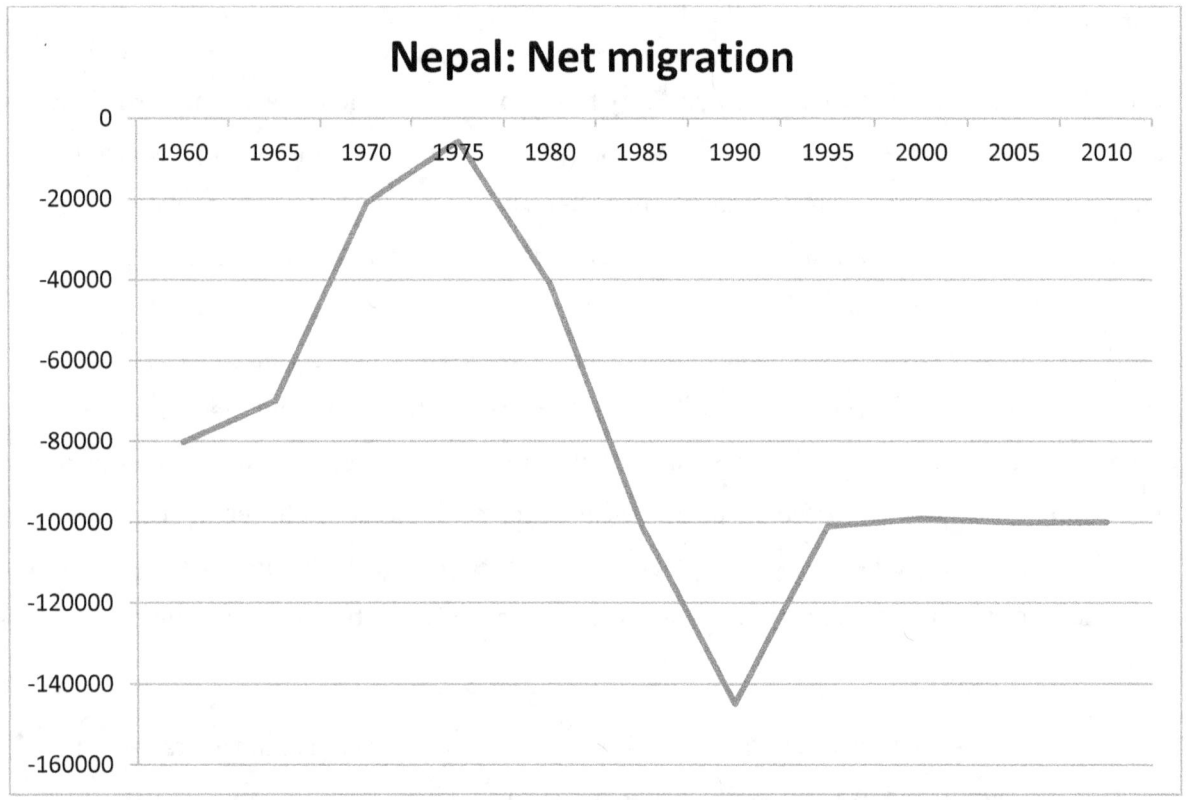

Source: World Bank Databank

Despite the decline in actual numbers of Gurkha recruits coming to Britain, now that their terms and conditions have changed, they are settling permanently in Britain. In 1984 Böhning (cited in Castles & Miller, 1998, p28) summarised four sequential stages of migration and its eventual lead to assimilation or the formation of ethnic groups within a receiving country.

1) Temporary labour migration of young workers, remittance of earnings and continued orientation to the homeland.
2) Prolonging of stay and the development of social networks based on kinship or common area of origin and the need for mutual help in the new environment.

3) Family reunion, growing consciousness of long-term settlement, increasing orientation towards the receiving country, and emergence of ethnic communities with their own institutions (associations, shops, cafes, agencies, professions).

4) Permanent settlement which, depending on the actions of the government and population of the receiving country, leads either to secure legal status and eventual citizenship, or to political exclusion, socioeconomic marginalisation and the formation of permanent ethnic minorities.

Following the decision to allow the Gurkhas to settle in Britain at the end of their army service (UK Border Agency) stage 3 of this model has been reached. Tensions are being felt in Aldershot where it is estimated 10,000 of them have settled and are building new lives (BBC News, 2011). The future nature of the Gurkhas relationship with Nepal and how they can continue to assist and develop their home country is the subject of the rest of this paper.

2.2 THE EFFECTS OF MIGRATION ON HOME COUNTRIES

Early attempts to understand the impact of migration on home countries have generally concluded that the effect of international migration was negative for productivity and economic growth. Terms such as 'brain drain' were coined and utilised in the belief that the loss of human capital abroad was not compensated by any other benefit such as remittances.

The expression 'brain drain' was conceived by the British Royal Society to describe the loss of skilled workers from Europe to the United States after the Second World War (Gibson & McKenzie, 2011). The term gained currency, yet by 1965 was critiqued, first by Johnson (cited in Gibson & McKenzie, 2011, p107) for being overtly negative and for being "obviously a loaded phrase, involving implicit definitions of economic and social welfare, and implicit assertions about facts. This is because the term 'drain' conveys a strong implication of serious loss."

There is now a large volume of articles seeking to dispel the so-called brain drain myth; amongst them is a 2011 article by Gibson & McKenzie that aims to define the term unambiguously and to challenge many of the assumptions that go with it. They analyse the impact of skilled migration in particular and conclude that although migrants in the last decade have had higher skill levels than those before them, education levels in sending countries are also higher than they have been, and so in many cases there is no skill gap left behind.

In fact experience in Nepal directly verifies this assertion and an unpublished article (Shrestha, 2010) observes a correlation between demand for higher academic standards in new Gurkha recruits by the British Army and increased levels of school enrolment in the areas from which they are recruited. Shrestha (p25) writes "when the change in educational requirement occurred in 1993, young Gurkha ethnic men who were enrolled in school during that time responded by demanding more education in expectation of later serving in the British Gurkha Army". Of course not all those men who hoped to enter the army were able to, and so the education levels of those who remained in Nepal were raised as well, to the benefit of the country more generally.

Docquier and Rapoport (2011) have produced a discussion paper for the Institute of the Study of Labor (IZA) that analyses the relationship between brain drain and development. The article's conclusion is more pessimistic about the increasingly dominant form of highly skilled migration that is taking place and it warns that brain drain is a serious cause for concern for developing countries. The paper demonstrates how the movement of highly skilled migrants is 'making human capital scarcer where it is already scarce and more abundant where it is already abundant, thereby contributing to increasing inequality' on a global scale (p50-51). Though this is the general pattern, the article emphasises that this need not be the case and highlights certain countries that have been able to 'seize the global benefits from having a skilled, educated Diaspora'; these include China, India, Indonesia and Brazil (ps 25 & 51).

Since the 1960s, when the term 'brain drain' was first criticised, its opposite 'brain gain' has been used and applied as a way to define a receiving country's benefit from migration. India has gone one step further and has successfully harnessed its Diaspora in order to benefit itself, particularly within the IT sector (Docquier & Rapoport, 2011). In 2010 Indian Prime Minister Dr Manmohan Singh celebrated the reversal of "brain drain" to "brain gain". He highlighted the flood of skilled workers back to India and said that "we are drawing on the global 'brain bank' of people of Indian origin worldwide" (Government of India, 2010).

As figure 2 demonstrates, the amount received by Nepal in remittance income is rising rapidly yet there is a dearth of articles available analysing in detail how Gurkha recruitment and remittances have impacted upon the economic and social make-up of Nepal. The evidence is instead on the ground in the form of wealthy towns and districts from which the Gurkhas have traditionally been recruited, for example Pokhara and Dharan (Jolly, 2009). Sapkota (2012) states that 'the indirect benefits received by districts from where most of the Gurkhas hail are tremendous. The British and Indian governments [both of which recruit Gurkhas to serve in their respective armies] have been investing a huge sum of money in social welfare of the relatives of Gurkhas and their hometowns. They have invested in agriculture, healthcare, education, and infrastructure, among others'. Yet it is these same regions that have been most impacted by not only the loss of an able workforce, but also by the remittance income that is returned in its place. The article also hints that additional aid, than it might otherwise receive, may be contributed by the British Government to Nepal because the Gurkhas are serving in their national army.

Figure 2: Remittances to Nepal

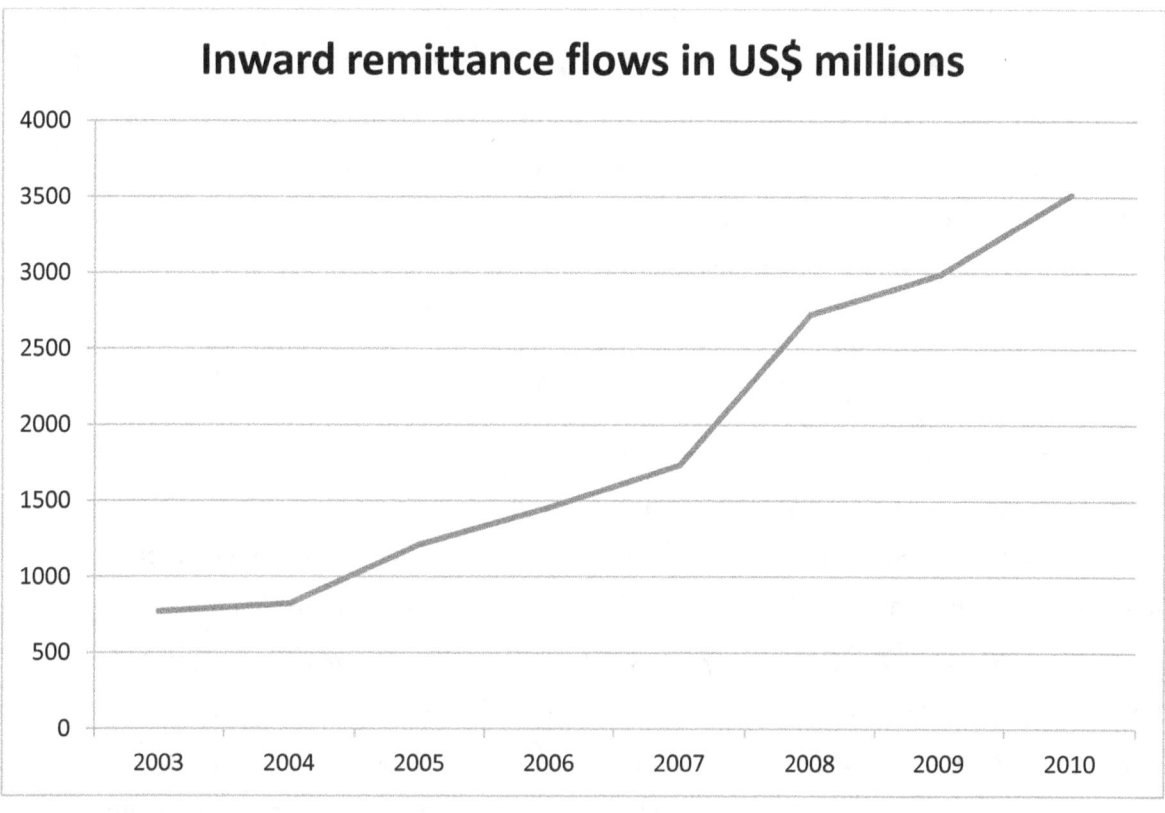

Source: Migration and Remittances Factbook 2011, World Bank

Sapkota (2012) puts forward a forceful argument urging the Nepali government to continue to allow Gurkha recruitment because of the positive effect it has on the country. The article, published in a Nepali newspaper, gives three main reasons for this. The first of these is economic; Gurkha remittance income is a key source of foreign exchange and reaches Nepal through formal channels. These formal channels are being promoted to all overseas workers by the Nepali government so that the benefit of remittance income to the country as a whole can be maximised. Secondly, Sapkota contends that Gurkha recruitment has become a part of the Nepali caste and tribal systems; if recruitment were stopped it would foster ethnic rivalries as particular tribes, such as the Gurungs, Rais and Limbus may feel especially disadvantaged by any prohibitive ruling. Finally Sapkota appeals to the sense of pride that Nepal has in its Gurkha soldiers and reminds the reader of the many awards Gurkha soldiers have won for their brave service. He concludes that they are a reason for the country to hold their heads high. This is in opposition to the Nepali Government conclusion that they are a source of shame because such a large group of Nepalis serve another's countries army and policies. In conclusion the article reasons that Gurkhas soldiers work under far better conditions and do far more to serve Nepal's interests than Nepali workers in the Gulf region and as such should be preferred.

2.3 DIASPORAS AND HOW BEST TO HARNESS THEM

Diaspora populations, as a subset of migrants, are increasingly being recognized by the World Bank as significant to development. The Migration and Remittances Unit at the bank, headed by Dilip Ratha (Lead Economist) has produced a series of articles that chart the increasingly positive perception of Diasporas. Ratha has produced a considerable number of practical papers over the last decade that discuss and recommend ways in which Diaspora groups can contribute towards home country economies particularly in Asia and Africa.

In 2011 Ratha and Plaza wrote a summary of their recommendations of the useful ways in which Diasporas contribute to home country development for the International Monetary Fund; the article is a useful list of ideas, each of which may be applied to Gurkhas. The first and largest portion of the paper highlights the positive impact of remittances and the stabilising effect these have on home countries as remittance flows increase when 'the recipient country is in an economic downturn or experiences a disaster' (p49). Diasporas also increase trade and investment as they often prefer to buy home goods and seek out ways of importing and distributing them in the country in which they have settled, all to the benefit of the home country. Beyond this, some embassies have organised their Diasporas to provide overseas market information through the creation of Diaspora trade councils, trade missions and business networks. Some Diaspora may even have surplus capital to invest in home country business start-ups to enable them to take advantage of new markets; for instance 'emigrants may be more willing than other investors to take on risks in their origin country because they are better able to evaluate investment opportunities and possess contacts to facilitate the investment process' (p49).

Diaspora communities are increasingly being recognised as powerful political voices and some, particularly the Israeli Diaspora in the United States, have demonstrated their ability to affect international relations in favour of their home countries. The African Foundation for Development in the United Kingdom has successfully evolved new ideas and put pressure on the British government to transform policies and practices that have a bearing on Africa (Page & Mercer, 2012).

Ratha recommends Diaspora bonds in the 2011 paper for the IMF as having massive potential for raising finance for development projects. A Diaspora bond is 'a retail savings instrument marketed to Diaspora members' (p50) and is a means of leveraging the affluence of patriotic and financially savvy migrants for home country benefit. The bonds offer investors the chance to invest in their home country and capitalise on their desire to do good. In theory they have great potential for raising finance for development projects, in which migrants are interested, at home. For instance Diaspora fund income may be used to build schools, hospitals, power stations, roads and airports and are most successful when those projects are perceived to be of benefit to a migrant's home region. The advantages may not only be for development; Diaspora bonds, if used to generate sufficiently large amounts, can have a positive impact on a country's sovereign credit rating and will enhance the perception of the nation in world markets. However Ratha cautions that Diaspora investors will be deterred from risking their hard-earned capital if home countries are perceived to lack proper governance or experience ongoing civil strife; this may be a problem for many developing countries, including Nepal. Interest in purchasing Diaspora bonds also dwindles over time and first-generation immigrants are generally likely to invest more, even though the second generation is usually better off (Ketkar & Ratha, 2007).

Ratha also heads and contributes to a blog on the World Bank website entitled 'People Move: a blog about migration remittances and development'. Nepal features in discussions about Diaspora bonds intermittently and is first mentioned explicitly by Ratha (though only in the footnotes) in a 2011 discussion paper in which it is noted that Nepal as a country 'can potentially consider Diaspora bonds' (Ratha, Mohapatra & Scheja, 2011). Yet in January 2011 the People Move blog was already asking questions about what had happened to the Foreign Employment Bond (that has similar characteristics to a Diaspora Bond) that Nepal launched to raise revenues. Nepal's foreign employment bond is a form of specialist Diaspora bond and can only be purchased by overseas earnings; until 2011 it had only been made available for purchase by the Nepali Diaspora working in Qatar, Saudi Arabia, UAE, and Malaysia.

Several articles consider case study countries and illustrate in detail how their Diasporas have been used to further development. The merits of Diasporas bonds and how they have been utilised by the respective Governments of Israel and India are explored specifically and provide useful illustrations though the two countries have made use of them for different purposes (Ketkar & Ratha, 2007). Israel is hugely reliant on its Diaspora, especially those in the United States, as a source of overseas borrowing; the Bank of New York is the sole fiscal agent. Bonds are issued in accordance with the government's foreign exchange requirements and in 2005 the bonds made up 32 percent of the Israeli government's outstanding debt. Revenue has been used to 'finance major public sector projects such as desalination, construction of housing and communication infrastructure' (p7). The bond has been so successful because Israel pursued a determined sales strategy; after the Second World War a coast-to-coast tour of the USA was used to generate interest and sales. Today regular investor events in Jewish communities continue to produce regular and reliable high sales, yet bond purchasers do not need to be of Israeli origin, a key difference between the Israeli bonds and those issued by Nepal.

India, on the other hand, has made use of Diaspora bonds to raise revenue on a sporadic basis and has only issued them on three separate occasions each of which was in relation to crises in overseas funding flows (Ketkar & Ratha, 2007). The State Bank of India (SBI) has limited bond sales to Non-resident Indians, yet it is unclear why this restriction has been imposed. Ketkar and Ratha speculate that the SBI may have done this to increase sales because 'Indian investors would be more eager to invest in instrument that are available exclusively to them' or could it be that 'Indian Diaspora investors would show more understanding and forbearance that other investors if India encountered a financial crisis' (p11). No matter which reason is correct, the Indian Diaspora bond has a successful track record and Nepal would do well to learn from its neighbour.

Docquier and Rapoport (2011) provide detail about how the Indian Diaspora in Silicon Valley in particular has contributed to the rise of India's vibrant IT sector; in fact they state that 'it is now common to celebrate the contribution of the Indian Diaspora to the country's industrial and economic success' (p41). In the article Docquier and Rapoport analyse how migrants reduce transaction costs and facilitate 'the diffusion of knowledge and ideas, highly-skilled Diasporas settled in the developed countries encourage technology diffusion, stimulate trade and FDI and contribute to improving domestic institutions'. For instance 27 percent of Indian entrepreneurs in Silicon Valley regularly exchange information on jobs, business opportunities and technology with people back home (Saxenian 2002, cited in Docquier & Rapoport, 2011). Likewise the positive perception of Indian migrants in the US inspired a demand for them in other countries (e.g. Germany & Japan) that had not accepted migrants from India previously. As Indian software engineers were increasingly sought for, this virtuously increased the number of students in India wishing to study IT and academic levels across the country have risen. Moreover, Diaspora groups have been critical in the formation of sectoral representative bodies; groups of aspiring entrepreneurs have successfully lobbied 'for a better framework for entrepreneurship in India' and have helped to 'change the regulatory framework for venture capital'.

In a recent article, Page and Mercer (2012) challenge the two current dominant approaches to managing Diaspora behaviour and suggest that the everyday life of Diaspora members is more significant to home country development than externally recommended initiatives. The first approach to be dismissed is the view that diasporas are 'decision makers' and the associated assumption that 'diasporas need help from the development establishment to make the most efficient choices about the way they remit' (p4). This view also assumes that 'the role of government ... in this scenario is to help educate the Diaspora about the consequences of their choices or steer them in particular directions' (p5). By far the largest speculation made by this approach is that the 'Diaspora will change their behaviour in response to these stimuli' and as such it is dismissed (p5).

The second approach that the article gives little credence to is the concept of diasporas as 'option-setters' whereby they 'contribute to the process of generating the list of options for remitting from which individuals make their choices' (p6). This process relies upon 'organic intellectuals of the Diaspora [to] evolve new ideas and campaigns to put pressure on the British government to reform their policies and practices' and observes that these individuals 'become enrolled into the policy-making process' (p7). Brinkerhoff (2011) also cautions NGOs and governments against instrumentalising Diasporas, and would rather see them embraced as independent partners in the development process. The key criticism of both these approaches is that they 'both treat diasporas as agglomerations of autonomous individuals and draw on ideas of economic rationality to explain the choices those individuals make' (p7).

The paper proposes as an alternative to these two an approach to the Diaspora that views it as a 'community of practice' in which the dualism between individuals and their communities is better explained and reflected. The practice of remitting is therefore better regarded as 'a routinised form of behaviour' (p8) and 'is acquired through the experience of being socialized within it [the Diaspora community]' (p9). Remitting to the home country therefore may be simultaneously perceived by the Diaspora as the right and proper thing to do yet may be carried out begrudgingly. In order to maximize the impact the Diaspora makes on home country development Page & Mercer therefore suggest that their lifestyles and habits are analysed and routine events such as weddings and holidays in the home country are examined for their potential to contribute. The paper concludes with a call for more research in this area.

2.4 POLICIES TO MAXIMISE THE DEVELOPMENT BENEFITS OF DIASPORAS

In their discussion paper for the Institute for the Study of Labor (IZA), Docquier & Rapoport (2011) suggest three policy areas that could be adapted to maximize the home-country return from Diaspora and migrant populations. These three are Education, Emigration and Taxation policies; also considered is the Immigration policy of receiving countries.

In the case of Education policy the article suggests that the governments of migrant sending countries can choose to spend public money on 'internationally transferable education (e.g. exact sciences, engineering, economics, medical professions)' or on 'country specific skills (e.g. law)' (p44). Should a country choose to focus on educating students with country specific skills, then it runs the risk of not having enough engineers etc. of its own to draw on. This situation should be avoided therefore and the paper recommends that both transferable and country-specific education is promoted. They suggest that the numbers of graduates remaining in a source nation is kept sufficiently high enough to meet the needs of the source country by the introduction of a graduate-migrant tax. The tax may act as a deterrent for those seeking work abroad if raised in response to skill short-falls at home.

A tax on emigrants was first proposed over thirty years ago by Jagdesh Bhagwati, an Indian born economist and himself an emigrant (Docquier & Rapoport, 2011). It remains somewhat controversial and has been criticized as a form of extortion; there is yet to be a successful tax policy implemented by a sending-country. In theory the tax would compensate home-countries for their loss of highly skilled citizens, especially if those people had benefitted from a state-provided education, and would bring about income equity for those left behind. However implementation of the tax is still problematic and issues such as which country would enforce the collection of such taxes are unresolved. Both sending and receiving countries could come to bilateral agreements – a very large number of which would be required to cover all country combinations; or an international authority could collect the taxes and return them to home nations. Taxation is increasingly seen as a development tool and as a means for ensuring good governance; if a country's government is to successfully tax its citizens or emigrants it needs to show an interest in them by collecting information about them, furthermore citizens that pay taxes are more likely to hold their governments to account for public services (Moore, 2001). Undoubtedly Diaspora members will be more likely to retain an interest in their home country if they are paying taxes to its government, yet such a tax would most certainly be unpopular.

Neither serving Gurkhas nor retired Gurkhas pay tax to the Nepali government, compensation for the loss of their citizens is instead a feature of the tripartite agreement between Nepal, Britain and India (who also recruits Gurkhas) and is soon to be usurped by an updated Memorandum of Understanding between Britain and Nepal (Ministry of Defence, 2012). The British Government is also firmly committed to improving the livelihoods of those left behind in the villages from which Gurkhas are traditionally recruited and through the Gurkha Welfare Scheme 'provides aid to Gurkha ex-servicemen, their dependants and communities, including running residential homes for the elderly, providing medical help, and building health and educational facilities'. The scheme is funded by both the public and DfID and forms part of the UKs overall commitment to Nepal whereby 'between now and 2015, the UK Government's programme across Nepal will work to ensure that 230,000 direct jobs are created through private sector development, 4,232 kilometres of roads are built or upgraded, and 110,000 people benefit from improved sanitation. In addition, we will help four million Nepalis strengthen their ability to cope with natural disasters and the adverse impact of climate change.' (Ministry of Defence, 2012).

In the concluding remarks of the article written by Gibson and Mckenzie (2011, p126) there is a challenge that is yet to be resolved: "if brain drain hinders development, then acting to limit brain drain should encourage development. But what are the actual effects of policy actions to reduce high-skilled immigration?"

On Emigration policy, Docquier & Rapoport (2011) demonstrate that immigration prospects abroad provide a powerful incentive for human capital accumulation in developing countries. If policy restrictions are placed on the international mobility of educated residents then the result is likely to be a long-term overall decrease in the human capital of home populations. The outcome is that residents of developing countries stagnate with nowhere to go and little incentive to improve themselves so that they can participate in the global skills market; Docquier & Rapoport (2011) call this 'brain waste'. Similarly the paper warns that immigration policies of receiving nations need to designed carefully so as not to 'contradict the objectives of their aid and development policies' (p47).

Policies to maximize the return from migrants and Diasporas are no substitute for domestic development policies and associated reforms (Khoudour-Castéras, 2007); they should not be viewed as a means of exporting problems. For instance 'the reduction of unemployment should be the result of an active job-creation policy, not of the mass departure of the unemployed' (p157). Page & Mercer (2012) also warn against the growing dependence of developing countries on remittances to drive development and highlight rising inequality and uneven development between those in receipt of remittances and those families that are not. During 2011 Nepal's GDP was $15,722 million of which $3,951 million (25%) was remittance income (World Bank, International Organisation for Migration). Consequently traditional caste divisions between people groups are being superseded by a new 'caste' system based on whether one has family overseas and access to remittance income. Khoudour-Castéras therefore concludes that 'migration has thus become a perverse process, creating "poverty traps" whereby flawed economic and social policies lead to increased migration to industrialized countries, which in turn makes it so governments do not feel the need to undertake the types of reforms required to overcome underdevelopment' (p157).

PART THREE: CATALOGUE OF SOLUTIONS

This section lists the possible ways in which the Gurkhas could contribute to Nepal's development and that the British Government could implement to make up for the loss Nepal is suffering now that the Gurkhas no longer return to the country. The ideas have been generated by the literature review and this section also introduces initiatives suggested by the Gurkhas themselves during a meeting with the Gurkha Major of the Queen's Own Gurkha Logisitc Regiment in Aldershot and in focus groups with 248 Gurkha Signal Squadron in Stafford. During the research time in Stafford serving soldiers participated in one focus group discussion and their wives took part in another.

3.1 ADVOCACY & LOBBYING ON BEHALF OF NEPAL

As both Page & Mercer (2012) and Ratha & Plaza (2011) acknowledge, Diaspora groups are increasingly being recognized as a political voice for their home countries. In order to speak at the appropriate level and with the needed expertise the Gurkha Diaspora will need to evolve 'organic intellectuals' (Page & Mercer, 2012, p7) who can not only identify the issues but also discern and articulate their solutions.

Both the men's and women's focus groups were asked to suggest specific Nepali policy areas in which they would like to see reform. The men's group joked that they were overwhelmed with all the problems they could see in Nepal and the change they thought was necessary; they didn't know where to start! They were also quick to point out that they were very busy and therefore not able to involve themselves in matters much beyond their own careers. However, they could suggest other Nepalese groups that were involved in reform and were developing a nascent voice for the Gurkhas in the UK. These were the British Gorkha Army Ex-Servicemen Organisation (BGAESO, 2012) and The British Gurkha Welfare Society (BGWS, 2012) both of which do speak out on behalf of Gurkhas but in their own interest rather than to serve Nepal more generally. Self interest is evident in the BGWS's own motto which is 'Society of the Gurkhas, by the Gurkhas, for the Gurkhas'. Following the success of the BGWS in securing equal pension rights and settlement for Gurkhas in the UK, it should consider using its power to lobby on behalf of the oppressed in Nepal.

The Non-Resident Nepali association was also suggested and has a far better track record of lobbying for reform in Nepal as it unites the global Nepali Diaspora; its egalitarian maxim is 'For Nepali, by Nepali' (NRN UK, 2012). The headquarters are in Kathmandu and there is a British National Coordination council that bases itself in London. None of the Gurkhas in the meetings were aware of what issues NRN UK were seeking to address and they also pointed out that the council in the UK was made up of rich, high caste Nepalis. Whether this stereotype is correct is uncertain; however there was a definite reluctance to be involved with them. Yet, by uniting themselves with a well coordinated and resourced body, whose broad aims seem to be in the interest of Nepal, Gurkhas may begin to understand some of the issues that Nepal faces and feel less overwhelmed by them.

Two specific issues that Gurkhas may wish to speak out on and which affect Nepal negatively were raised in the focus groups; these were environmental change and people trafficking. Once again the soldier's group seemed both to be unaware of advocacy in general and in how they may be involved. It was put forward that environmental organizations, in their campaign activities, often looked for native people to speak out on behalf of countries affected by climate change, of which Nepal is one. One of the younger soldiers showed an interest in doing this, yet he clearly did not know any environmental groups to approach. There is an opportunity here for Gurkhas to identify existing groups that campaign on issues that affect their home communities and for campaign organizations to recruit campaigners from Diaspora groups.

In the discussion on human trafficking in the wives group there was a high level of awareness of the problem and strong feelings for it to be stopped. The women were able to share stories of organ taking and the disappearance of street children that they had heard. One lady had studied social work in Kathmandu (before marrying and moving to England) and had first-hand knowledge of the issues. All the women felt powerless to help, however, and somewhat nervous about doing so also. It was suggested that they could visit villages, on their return trips to Nepal, to warn the villagers about the dangers of trafficking and of travelling away with men on their own to be forced into prostitution. Trafficking groups in Nepal are organized by a kind of mafia and the women knew that action to stop trafficking would be risky. The wives also felt that if they travelled to a village outside the area in which they were from, the female residents of that village would not listen to their warnings about trafficking. The wives did agree if they could at least warn women from their own villages, and possibly the wider district, about trafficking this would be better than doing nothing.

3.2 REMITTING FINANCES THROUGH CHARITIES

The advantage of the Gurkhas sending funds back to Nepal via UK registered charities is that an additional 25% is contributed by the British Government with any donation. This therefore increases the value of the donation and therefore the total amount that may be received in Nepal. For example if a Gurkha currently remits £100 back home, if administered by a charity it would instead be worth £125 to the country. This however assumes the charity has no or low overheads; if the overheads were at least smaller than the 25% added, there would still be a net benefit to Nepal.

All of the Gurkhas at the meetings regularly sent money back home to extended families, most commonly to pay for schooling for nieces and nephews. Nonetheless payments such as these could not be channelled through a charity because all UK charities have a statutory requirement to demonstrate Public Benefit so that 'the opportunity to benefit must not be unreasonably restricted' (Charity Commission, 2012). Were the Gurkhas to switch their support to directly funding the schools that their family members attended then there would be an opportunity to channel their remittances through a charity and gift aid could be claimed. The transaction may become clouded and open to abuse however because the school in question would presumably then be expected to educate their niece or nephew for free in exchange for the charitable contributions. There are disadvantages to organising all remittance flows through formal channel, such a charities, because informal methods of transferring money to family are often more flexible, quicker and often more reliable (Agunias, 2009, cited in Page & Mercer, 2012)

There was general enthusiasm from the Gurkhas for supporting schools in their home villages and financing infrastructure projects such as toilets, libraries and wells. Almost all of them had contributed to such projects that had been organised by Gurkhas in the UK in response to the needs of home villages. Many had taken part in the Trailwalker event to raise funds for the Gurkha Welfare Trust, yet it was unclear if funds raised for smaller projects had been raised through a charity and whether rules for repayment of gift aid had been taken advantage of. The Gurkhas would benefit from general awareness raising about the role of charities and gift aid rules so that future projects could be set up to maximize the value of funds raised and also to guard against misappropriation.

Many Gurkhas though were fed up with their home villages asking for money from them and were sick of being perceived as 'cash cows'. One man even described how his village had commandeered family land from him for a communal village building in his absence. Another senior Gurkha vividly described how as soon as he stepped off the plane in Kathmandu he felt as if everybody he met was after his money. A sergeant, likely to be earning a little over £30,000 per annum, stated that for a typical trip home he felt socially obliged to take around £4000 worth of gifts. As a consequence of such feelings and experiences there was a desire from all of them for other ways in which they could contribute to Nepal's development from the UK rather than just financially. Given the increasing dependence of Nepal on Remittance income (see figure 2 above) this may be no bad thing; it would be in Nepal's interest to utilise its migrants in other ways rather than just for monetary gain. It needs to address issues in its domestic situation rather than view the solution to its problems as one of sending more and more citizens overseas to work, thus increasing its dependence on remittances further (Khoudour-Casteras, 2007).

3.3 DIASPORA BOND

As stated in the Literature Review above, Diaspora Bonds are in vogue with the World Bank and are perceived as having great potential for raising development finance.

In the focus group with the Gurkha soldiers no one present had heard of a Diaspora bond before. Once they had been explained, in theory the men were generally keen on the idea of contributing towards infrastructure projects at home and seeing a return on their investment; they stated that they could afford to invest greater amounts than they could afford to give to projects where there was no return (i.e. remit or donate). Many of them were saving for their post-Army careers and hypothetically viewed a Diaspora bond as a suitable investment. As to where they would prefer their money to go, popular infrastructure projects were hydro-power, transport and they had a bias towards regional projects rather than Nepal-wide initiatives. However, they had serious misgivings about whether monies invested in a Diaspora bond would reach the projects they were intended for, in which case they were not keen to invest. They pointed out that without a constitution Nepal did not appear to them to be a wise investment right now and they felt their money was safer elsewhere (presumably in UK banks). There were also concerns about corruption and the misappropriation of funds, to mitigate this risk they thought a guarantee to return the funds from the institution managing the bond would be prudent. Nonetheless, one Gurkha stated that even if funds went missing he would still be glad that they were missing in Nepal where they would at least benefit someone there, rather than elsewhere!

At the meeting with the Gurkha wives they were also theoretically welcome to the idea of a Diaspora bond but they too had qualms about corruption and the embezzlement of funds by middlemen. They could cite examples of road building projects in Nepal where cement had gone missing and new houses had sprung up instead for local elites. They were also concerned about increasing inequality in Nepal and feared that investing in a Diaspora bond may exacerbate this inequality. It was suggested that a private investment fund may be more successful than a Government managed fund at preventing corruption and misappropriation. Management by a private body may also ensure the infrastructure works in which the fund was investing were carried out on time and in budget. Therefore the return on investment would be better guaranteed.

During a meeting with Mahesh Bhattarai, Executive Director of Public Debt Management at Nepal Rastra Bank (the national bank of Nepal) in June further questions were asked about Nepal's experiences and objectives in issuing a Diaspora Bond. Nepal has issued a Foreign Employment Bond, its version of a Diaspora Bond, twice in the past and in 2012 has made it available for purchase in the UK for the first time. It must be paid for in Nepali Rupees, though proof that those monies were earned overseas is required at the time of purchase. It is therefore not a means of raising foreign exchange as done so by other nations, e.g. Israel and India (Ketkar & Ratha, 2007).

The Foreign Employment Bonds are set to give a fixed rate return between 9.5% and 10.5% per annum and are issued annually. However the issue period is only short; less than three weeks which this year ran from 24th June to 10th July. The bank aimed to raise 1 billion Nepali Rupees, equivalent to £7.4 million, from the bond sale. Supposedly funds raised by the bond will be spent on productive capital goods including roads, irrigation, hydro-power and telecoms, though the final decision would rest with the Government of Nepal and the power to choose where the funds were spent was theirs. When asked if Nepal Rastra Bank had any legal recourse if the Government did not spend the funds appropriately, Mr Bhattarai could only laugh, implying that there was little transparency between the Government and the national bank and no legal powers to ensure agreements between them were adhered to. Given that the country is currently without a constitution this is a further indicator that the Government may not be a worthy guardian of any funds raised at the present time.

Responsibility for selling and marketing the bond had been outsourced to a number of sales agencies including International Money Exchange (IME) and City Express Money Transfer Pvt, amongst others. During the interview it was inferred that these agencies had representative offices in the UK that would administer all bond purchases, yet details provided after the interview by e-mail required Gurkhas to contact offices in Nepal if they wished to procure the bond.

When asked about the sales and marketing strategy of these agencies, Mr Bhattarai knew little and indicated that it was the responsibility of the appointed agencies to carry out all sales and marketing activity. Having spoken to Gurkhas in this country it was already clear that they would prefer to invest in regional infrastructure projects. Nepal Rastra Bank has not carried out any market research of its own to understand what Diaspora members wish to invest in and thus enable it to market the bond more successfully.

Nepal Rastra Bank does not have the monopoly on bond issues in the country and thought that private banks could probably issue bonds as well if they so chose, no examples were given though. Mr Bhattarai also cited Nepal Electric who regularly issue Power Bonds that are available to all investors with a Nepali bank account, not just overseas workers.

Neither of the Foreign Employment Bonds issued in the past raised anywhere near the amount that was hoped for. In fact Nepal's only successful bond issue was in the wake of the 1985 earthquake to raise emergency finance and was available to all its citizens. It seems therefore that Nepal Rastra Bank has little chance of raising the entire 1 billion Nepali Rupees that is its aim, yet there was little desire to alter its strategy. Israel has had huge success with its own Diaspora bond due in no small part to a tour of the U.S. by Israeli politicians, including the then Prime Minister, with the express purpose of selling the bond (Ketkar & Ratha, 2007). The suggestion that Mr Bhattarai might tour the UK to drum up support for the Foreign Employment Bond was perceived as far too expensive, though surely the increase in awareness and sales the tour would generate would likely pay for itself. When asked what would happen if the entire one billion rupees was not raised, Mr Bhattarai quite simply stated that the Nepalese treasury would cover the deficit and could do so because it was full. This was a staggering statement, not only in relation to the Diaspora bond and why therefore Nepal Rastra Bank was bothering to go through the rigmarole of issuing them, but also in relation to the entire country. Mr Bhattarai's opinion was that the Government thought the country currently too unstable to spend the money in the treasury on its own people, despite their poverty. In light of this, the question posed by Page & Mercer (2012) that asks 'why should development at home become the responsibility of those who have migrated?' (p12) is well justified. Encouraging Gurkhas to invest in a somewhat risky bond when the Government of Nepal is not spending the funds it already has is illogical.

3.4 DISASTER RESPONSE

Nepal is vulnerable to earthquakes and a 'big one' is past due, the capital Kathmandu is one of the most vulnerable cities in the world with an overdue earthquake predicted to kill tens of thousands of people (Taggart, 2011). The idea that the Gurkhas, serving or retired, could become involved after a disaster in Nepal would utilise their particular skills and experience in the Army and it distinguishes them from other Diaspora groups. For instance, Gurkha Signallers could help set up communications, Gurkha Engineers could assist in a multitude of scenarios and those from the Queen's Own Gurkha Logistic Regiment could potentially help aid reach remote areas. These areas of expertise, when combined with their ability to speak the local language, may be of much help in the wake of a natural catastrophe in Nepal.

Research shows that anyone with family members who have been affected by a disaster will find it very hard to carry out their duties whilst resisting the urge to find their relatives (Leurs & van Eekelen, 2012). Therefore Gurkhas may be best suited to giving assistance after an interval of time, such as a month or six weeks has passed after a disaster, rather than responding immediately. This would be at a point when the country is ready to be rebuilt and could make more use of their specialist skills.

During the focus group meeting those Gurkhas in attendance felt that helping after a disaster may be something they would like to do, however they doubted its cost-effectiveness. They thought it would only be worth returning to help if they could be certain their unique skills could be used, otherwise why not just organize local Nepali residents to help with rebuilding? However, they also suggested that they could be used to train the local police and army in responding to disasters. They did not believe they could respond in any way by themselves and would need to be 'led'.

The proposal that the Gurkhas could help in the wake of a disaster in Nepal is nascent and therefore undeveloped. Yet there appears to be some mileage in it and the advice of agencies who would act for the UK following a disaster in Nepal should be sought next. Devising a plan in consultation with those agencies, the British Army and the Gurkhas themselves would maximize their efficacy post-disaster. Making some soldiers available to the Gurkha Welfare Trust, with the permission of the British Government, to assist in their disaster response could be a first step towards this. Given the shift in emphasis from disaster response to preparedness this plan ought to be arranged as soon as feasibly possible (Leurs & van Eekelen, 2012). Furthermore, it is likely that, given the public support for Gurkhas in the UK, a natural disaster in Nepal could generate a large amount of funding. A strategy for collecting and coordinating those funds and whether they could be allocated to support either serving or retired Gurkhas in assisting Nepal to recover should also be considered.

3.5 TRADE WITH NEPAL

Gurkhas could enhance trade between Britain and Nepal at several levels. On a small-scale an individual or group of them could establish a business to import and sell Nepali goods. Of all the ideas discussed at the meeting with the Gurkha wives, this met with the greatest enthusiasm. The wives knew of many fair-trade craft co-operatives in Nepal and knew that their orders would provide valuable income for the small-scale producers in them. Items they considered worth importing were pashmina scarves, jewellery and other handicrafts. The women were also aware of local craft fairs in the Stafford area where the goods could be sold. Not only could they see the advantages of trading with Nepal in this way, they also understood that little capital would be required from them to set up such businesses and thus the concept was deemed accessible.

Some obstacles to the set up of such businesses were mentioned and these were unfamiliarity with customs rules and regulations and the high costs of postage between Nepal and the UK.

They suggested that perhaps the British Forces Postal Office (BFPO) could be utilized to send and receive items. To address customs issues and give advice about starting up small businesses either the Business Advice team from Stafford Borough Council or representatives from the nationwide Business Link initiative could be invited to provide training to the wives about how to take their trading ideas forward.

The United Kingdom is among the top ten trading partners of Nepal; therefore at a higher level Gurkhas may have something to offer (Embassy of Nepal, 2011). Ratha (2011) describes how 'some governmental agencies and private firms in African countries are tapping their diasporas to provide market information about the countries in which emigrants now live" (p49). These trade councils are most often organized by home country embassies that facilitate the involvement of their Diaspora. Amongst the products that Nepal exports to Britain are woollen carpets, handicrafts, ready-made garments, silverware and jewellery, leather goods, Nepali paper and paper products. During the meeting with the Gurkha wives they were keen to find out how they could help their embassy and what market information it requires, they expressed a need to be paid for any involvement however. The rise in the number of fair-trade goods in the UK was noted, yet they thought Nepal was lagging behind in its conversion to fair-trade mass production. Two of them came from villages where jute and cardamom were grown. In their experience as shoppers they had noticed a rise in the number of fair-trade spices but had yet to see fair-trade cardamom, perhaps Nepal could fill this gap?

The Embassy of Nepal in London maintains a list of Nepalese organizations in the UK (Embassy of Nepal, 2012) some of which focus on representing Nepali businesses in the UK and some that appear to pass on advice back to Nepal. The purpose of the list is far from clear, however, and certainly more could be done to make the Gurkha community aware of the wider Nepali Diaspora and how they could assist Nepali trade with the UK. Representatives from Nepal's Government in Kathmandu pledged to mobilize their Diaspora at the Consultation on South Asian Research, Education and Innovation coordinated by the World Bank (World Bank South Asia, 2011). To do this there needs to be a regular meeting between interested Gurkhas and their Embassy who should be facilitating their Diaspora to Nepal's advantage.

3.6 SPORT

This development solution was an idea raised by the Gurkha Major (GM) in Aldershot and reflects his own ambitions to see Nepal participating in international sporting events and thereby giving Nepalis a reason to be proud. He believed that citizens from his own home town of Jomsom would make excellent runners and, in much the same way as runners from rural Kenya have dominated international running competitions, he believed athletes from Jomsom could do likewise. In the 2012 Olympics Nepal's team consists of just ten people and in 2008 there were only eight. Clearly sport in Nepal would benefit from investment and the GM's vision was to spend time there training athletes, though it was unclear whether to do this he intended to settle in Nepal permanently or not. Therefore the solution may not be a strictly Diaspora led initiative; nevertheless a small team of permanent staff in Nepal could be supported by Diaspora members who could return to give training and pass on their skills. Fundraising for the project could also be carried out by the Diaspora.

The UK's Department for International Development has experience in supporting sports programmes in many third world countries; these include the Africa Sports and Talents Empowerment Programme (A-STEP) and the department has lent it's support to 1GOAL FIFA that aims to keep up the pressure to see primary schooling made freely available to every child. The links between sport, health and wellbeing have long been known; the emphasis is now also on sport as a tool for promoting education and developing leadership, as well as resolving conflict (Wroe & Doney, 2010). Those Gurkhas with a vision for using sport in Nepal as an instrument for development would benefit from learning from existing programmes elsewhere and working in partnership with funding organisations to see their visions become reality.

3.7 INVOLVEMENT WITH THE WIDER DEVELOPMENT COMMUNITY

Quite apart from the obvious language skills, retired Gurkhas, and in the future their children, have a lot to offer the development community. They have experience of living in two continents and many will have seen the development community in action in Afghanistan, Iraq and if they have served long enough, in Bosnia also. The development sector therefore is not unfamiliar to them and they are themselves accustomed to working for a large organisation.

The serving Gurkhas had not previously given any thought to returning to Nepal with a development organisation and neither had their wives. They were neither for nor against the idea and simply did not know whether living in Nepal, as a British development agency employee, would be feasible; consequently they were unable to make a decision as to their thoughts about doing so. Given that most development agencies require at least a bachelor's degree in a related subject it may be that Gurkha children will have the greatest opportunity to work in the sector. When discussing the potential for their children to work in development there was a sharp divide in the feelings between the soldiers and their wives. The women felt it would be wonderful if their children could spend a gap year in Nepal, not only to assist the country but for cultural bonds between their children and their native country to be strengthened. This view is echoed by Ravindra Shakya, country director of Restless Development (formerly Student Partnership Worldwide) who believes Gurkha children have much to give and gain from spending time in Nepal and would regard them as suitable short term volunteer candidates (personal conversation). The soldiers meanwhile vehemently did not want their children to take a break from their studies to spend time in Nepal (or anywhere else). Once again they were not keen that their children work for development organisations and instead held traditional views about careers; they would like their children to become Doctors or Engineers in the UK.

As for volunteering in Nepal themselves, the Gurkha wives were keen that their trips back home were more useful to Nepal than currently, though family commitments would prevent them from formally volunteering. As described in sections 3.1 and 3.5 they were interested in warning their villages about the dangers of trafficking and using the trips to buy goods to import and sell in the UK on their return. Page & Mercer (2012) discuss the value of embedding practices that assist home countries in the everyday lifestyles of Diaspora members and it is these, the article argues, that have the most potential for engendering development. Any trip home by a Diaspora member acts on the social fabric and it is the accumulated impacts of these actions that can be viewed as developmental. Making the most of Gurkhas' trips home to Nepal will first require them to understand that their actions do have a bearing on Nepal's development and to this end they need to learn and understand more about development and what can be done by them to improve Nepal's situation. Both focus groups did express a desire to learn more about development and also considered it necessary to better understand why Nepal was so poor and what was holding it back. They were particularly keen to know about what they could do to help Nepal, particularly if they could give time and skills rather than money, and viewed the research discussions as just the first step. Regular articles in Gurkha journals about poverty and development may heighten awareness of the issues and reach the wider Gurkha community. Further talks and discussions with all those interested will then ensure the ideas for development planted in their minds by the focus groups are not lost.

3.8 POLICIES

The rationale for implementing a 'Bhagwati' or migrant tax is much the same as that for issuing a Diaspora bond, the purpose is to raise finance. It is difficult to confirm the current state of the treasury with the summary provided by Mr Bhattarai; Nepal Rastra Bank has only made available Economic Reports up to 2009 on its website (Nepal Rastra Bank, 2012). Figure 3 however shows data held by the World Bank that indicates that Nepal's national savings are accumulating rapidly and are not being spent.

Figure 3: Gross Savings in Local Currency Units as collated by the Economic Policy and Debt department

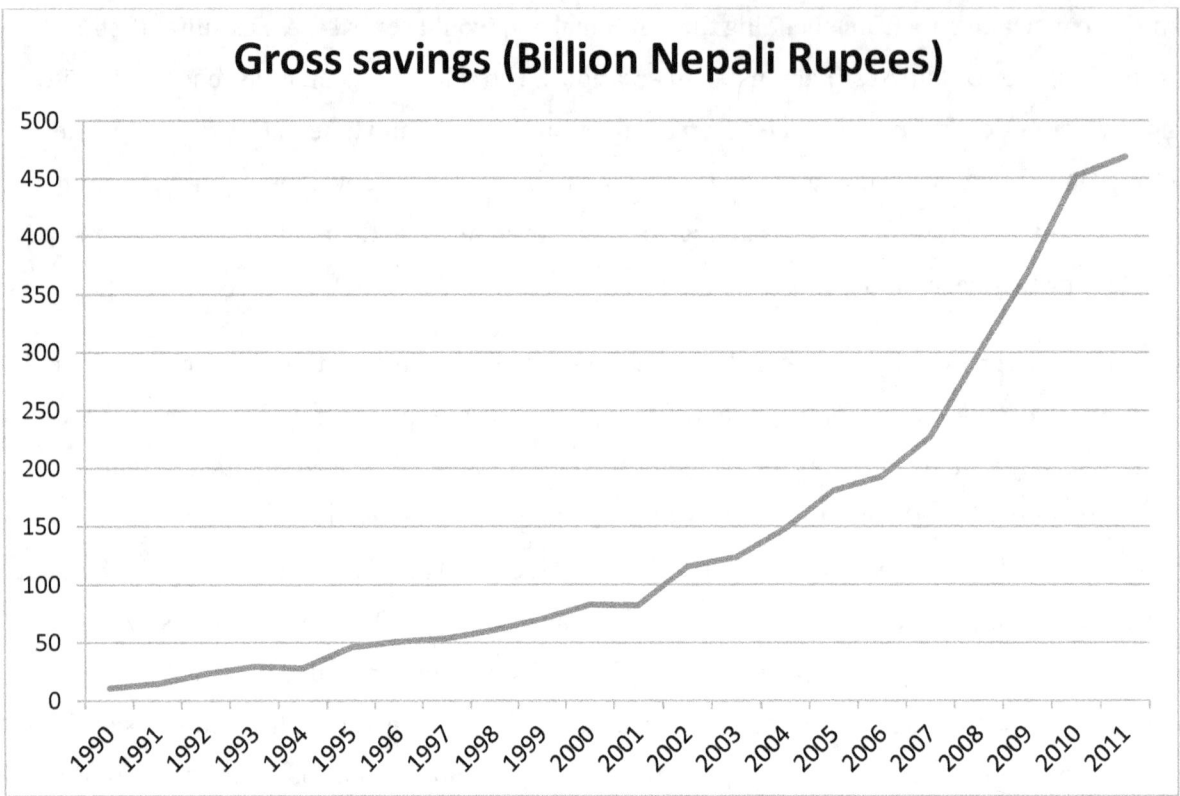

Gross savings (Billion Nepali Rupees)

Source: World Bank Databank

Were any attempt made by the Nepali Government to tax Gurkhas who choose to settle in the UK, the British Government ought to resist such efforts until it could be certain that the taxes paid will not be misappropriated and will be spent prudently in Nepal.

The criteria for the selection and recruitment of Gurkhas has been proved by Shrestha (2010) to impact on the education levels of the general population in Nepal. Any rise in standards expected by the British Army spurs all potential recruits to attain the new skill levels. Though the actual number of those recruited is small, there are many who train and aspire to be selected. In light of this the British Army needs to regularly review its recruitment criteria to ensure they are appropriate and set at a suitable level to inspire candidates to stay in education and become academically well-rounded and acquire useful new skills. For instance, if knowledge of first aid became a requirement, then many young men would be motivated to become proficient in it and the positive results may be widespread.

Key to maintaining links between a Diaspora and their home country is their ability to move freely and easily between the two countries. Bureaucratic barriers that artificially restrain not only their physical movement but the movement of their finances can erase the bonds between them and their home. This makes it less likely that they will act to encourage development in their home country. In order to maintain his 'Indefinite Leave to Remain' status a retired Gurkha must not stay away from Britain for more than two years. The result of this rule is that any Gurkha that wishes to stay in Nepal (whilst maintaining ILTR status) is deterred because flying back and forth to the UK from Nepal every two years is unaffordable for him. The rule has become an incentive to settle in the UK and does not allow Nepal to benefit from the return of some of their well trained and wealthy citizens who may wish to do so. Consequently the resettlement terms need to be reviewed so that Gurkhas who wish to remain in Nepal and contribute to its development from within the country are not dissuaded. Many of the Gurkhas at the focus groups did wish ultimately to settle in Nepal once their children had completed their education in Britain.

PART FOUR: SUMMARY OF RECOMMENDATIONS

4.1 Advocacy & Lobbying On Behalf Of Nepal

Create opportunities for Gurkhas and their wives to meet with existing pressure groups campaigning on issues related to Nepal.

Provide the Gurkha wives with information about human trafficking in Nepal so that they are better able to caution people from their home villages.

4.2 Remitting Finances through Charities

Identify UK based charities that are able to channel funds from Gurkhas to projects in Nepal that they wish to support, whilst complying with public benefit rules.

4.3 Diaspora Bond

Further examine the credit worthiness of Power Bonds and promote to Gurkhas if deemed worthy.

Approach private financial institutions to garner interest for creating a private Diaspora/Gurkha bond or similar investment instrument.

4.4 Disaster Response

Initiate a conversation between the Gurkhas and UK based emergency relief agencies to establish if they can be of help in the wake of a disaster in Nepal.

Consult with the Gurkha Welfare Trust to establish an emergency relief plan and consider giving permission for serving Gurkhas to participate in any emergency response.

Plan for how the Gurkhas could be utilised to raise funds in the UK following a disaster in Nepal.

4.5 Trade with Nepal

Provide small-business start up training, including information on importing and customs rules, to the Gurkha wives.

Invite the Embassy of Nepal to meet with retiring Gurkhas to explain how they may support trade between Nepal and the UK.

4.6 Sport

Create opportunities for interested Gurkhas to visit existing sports and development projects and give advice on how they may obtain funding for their own sports ideas.

4.7 Involvement with the Wider Development Community

Provide ongoing education on development to the Gurkhas and their wives through workshops and articles in Gurkha journals.

Establish a gap year programme for Gurkha children in Nepal in consultation with existing short-term programmes.

Establish a scholarship programme for Gurkha children who wish to study development at degree level or beyond.

4.8 Policies

Regularly review the British Army's recruitment criteria to ensure it motivates Nepali candidates to stay in education and acquire worthwhile skills.

Review the current rules pertaining to Indefinite Leave to Remain status so that Gurkhas can move freely between Britain and Nepal.

PART FIVE: CONCLUSION

Now that the Gurkhas have been granted settlement rights in the UK, they and their families are at the outset of a process of becoming increasingly orientated towards the UK and adopting it's lifestyles and values (Böhning, 1984 cited in Castles & Miller, 1998). It is at this juncture that habits are formed that will set the pattern for their ongoing involvement with Nepal and its development. These habits may have a greater effect on development in Nepal than any purposeful development interventions and since this is a period of rapid social change for them now is the time to act to influence it (Page & Mercer, 2012).

This paper has assumed that Gurkhas should help Nepal and is based on the moral position that because Nepal is poor and the actions of the Gurkhas can help to improve the living conditions there, then they should aid the country. It is part of an obligation all of us have to help those less fortunate than ourselves (Singer, 2009) and given that the Gurkhas know Nepal, as well as the idiosyncrasies that hold it back, they are better placed to assist it than others. Yet a question remains about how much help the Gurkhas should give to Nepal?

Without exception all of the Gurkhas and wives that took part in the focus groups and interviews had a strong desire to help Nepal and were already involved in doing so. Their attitudes and actions need to be celebrated and applauded; it is therefore not their values that need to be changed in the hope that their actions will modify as a result (Page & Mercer, 2012; Public Interest Research Centre, 2011). Gurkhas already hold strong values of benevolence and as a consequence it then becomes the responsibility of the governments of the UK and Nepal to foster policies and conditions that promote their generosity and magnanimity. In areas where the Gurkhas expressed interest in particular ideas and actions they should be encouraged to follow up on these and where possible given the resources to help them do so.

Making the most efficient use of what Gurkhas have to offer to Nepal does not involve simply providing them with a list of information and ways to spend their time and money in some vague hope that this will change their behaviour (Page & Mercer, 2012). Rather it is hoped that this paper will provide some useful pointers for the start of a conversation between the Gurkhas themselves, the British Army and the UK Government so that thinking about and acting to help Nepal can be done together and with the best advice. It is also the offer of a listening ear from the UK Government to hear their proposals and assist them as it can. It should not be forgotten that there are many pressures on Gurkhas to spend their money, in particular, on helping Nepal from family and villages back home and it is not the intention of this paper to add to those demands.

The famous quote by Anthropologist Margaret Mead: 'a small group of thoughtful people could change the world. Indeed, it's the only thing that ever has' is a reminder that it will most probably be the actions of a few Gurkhas that will inspire and motivate all of them to make the most meaningful changes. It is these few who will become those 'organic intellectuals' that Page & Mercer (2012) refer to and who are so key to developing new ideas and practices that shape the habits and lifestyles of the Diaspora community to which they belong. Of the two meetings held in Stafford it was the wives' meeting where the most energy for change and compassion for the issues in Nepal was found. Gurkha wives, like many Army wives, have long been overlooked, yet this initial research would suggest that it is they who have the most time and enthusiasm for the solutions developed here. The men, though frustrated that there were so many demands for their finances in Nepal, had little time to give in other ways to the country. Of the ideas discussed by the women they were most keen on three in particular. These were starting up small businesses to import Nepali goods, joining up with development organisations in Nepal during their trips back home, especially with their older children who would benefit from the cultural exchange and their most preferred option was to talk about these issues again and learn more about development. Quite simply they were excited and passionate about helping Nepal and this factor, more than anything written here, will be the driving force behind seeing the Gurkhas bring about positive change in Nepal.

REFERENCES

BBC News, 20 September 2011, **MP condemned for Gurkha 'asylum seeker' remarks** [online], http://www.bbc.co.uk/news/uk-14989700, accessed 14th May 2012

BGAESO [online] **British Gorkha Army Ex-Servicemen's Organisation**, http://bgaeso.org/, accessed 29th June 2012

BGWS [online] **British Gurkha Welfare Society**, http://bgws.org/, accessed 29th June 2012

Blakely, R (2009) Lumley's triumph could be Nepal's loss; Exit of affluent Gurkha veterans is feared, **The Times**, 29 July 2009

Brinkerhoff, J (2011) David and Goliath: Diaspora organizations as partners in the development industry, **Public Administration & Development**, Vol 31(1)

British Army (2012) **History of the Brigade of Gurkhas** [online] http://www.army.mod.uk/gurkhas/history.aspx, accessed 18th April 2012

Castles, S and Miller, M (1998) **The Age of Migration: International Population Movements in the Modern World**, Macmillan Press, Basingstoke, 2nd Edition

Charity Commission (2012) **Charities and Public Benefit** [online], http://www.charitycommission.gov.uk/Charity_requirements_guidance/Charity_essentials/Public_benefit/public_benefit.aspx#f3, accessed 3rd July 2012

Collier, P (2007) Migration and the Bottom Billion in **The Bottom Billion**, Oxford University Press

Docquier, F and Rapoport, H (2011) Globalization, Brain Drain and Development, **Institute for the Study of Labor (IZA) Discussion Paper No 5590**, Bonn

(The) Economist, Jul 30th 2009, **Gurkhas in Nepal: Old soldiers fade away**, from the print edition in Asia [online] http://www.economist.com/node/14140294, accessed 9th May 2012

(The) Economist, 19th Nov 2011, **The Magic of Diasporas**, Vol 400 (8760)

Embassy of Nepal (2011) **Nepal Britain Relations** [online], http://www.nepembassy.org.uk/nepal_britain_relations.php, accessed 9th July 2012

Embassy of Nepal (2012) Nepalese Organizations in the UK [online], http://www.nepembassy.org.uk/nep_orgs.php, accessed 9th July 2012

European External Action Service (2010) **Nepal: Country Strategy Paper 2007-2013 Mid-Term Review Document**, Indicative Programme 2011-2013, Brussels

Gibson, J and McKenzie, D (2011) Eight Questions about Brain Drain, **Journal of Economic Perspectives**, Vol 25 (Summer)

Government of India, (2010) **Hiren Mukherjee Memorial Lecture 2010** [online], Prime Minister's Office Press Release, December 2, http://pib.nic.in/release/release.asp?relid=68026 accessed 27th April 2012

Government of Nepal (2003) **The Tenth Plan (Poverty Reduction Strategy Paper) 2002–2007**, National Planning Commission, Kathmandu

Government of Nepal (2007) **Nepal: Poverty Reduction Strategy Paper Progress Report**, National Planning Commission, Kathmandu

Government of Nepal (2010) **Labour and Social Trends in Nepal 2010**, National Planning Commission, Kathmandu

Green, D (2012) **Daily Hansard - Written Answers** [online], http://www.publications.parliament.uk/pa/cm201212/cmhansrd/cm120315/text/120315w0002.htm#12031549001173, accessed 18th April 2012

Hatton, T and Williamson, J (1998) **The Age of Mass Migration: Causes and Economic Impact**, Oxford University Press, Oxford

International Organisation for Migration (2012) **Data for Nepal** [online] http://www.iom.int/jahia/Jahia/activities/nepal, accessed 27th June 2012

Jolly, J (2009) **Nepal town fears Gurkha exodus**, BBC News, Dharan

Ketkar, S and Ratha, D (2007) **Development Finance via Diaspora Bonds: Track record and Potential**, Paper presented at the Migration & Development Conference at the World Bank

Khoudour-Casteras, D (2007) International migration and development: the socioeconomic impact of remittances in Colombia, **CEPAL Review 92**, UN ECLAC

Leurs, R and Van Eekelen, W (2012) **Introductory notes on NGOs and disaster management**, University of Birmingham

Lokshin, M, Bontch-Osmolovski, M and Glinskaya, E (2010) Work-Related Migration and Poverty Reduction in Nepal, **Review of Development Economics**, Vol 14(2)

Massey, D, Axinn, W and Ghimire, D (2010) Environmental change and out-migration: evidence from Nepal, **Population and Environment**, Vol 32

Migration Information Source [online] www.migrationinformation.org, accessed 16th January 2012

Ministry of Defence (2012) **New support for Nepal's Gurkha communities** [online] http://www.mod.uk/DefenceInternet/DefenceNews/DefencePolicyAndBusiness/NewSupportF orNepalsGurkhaCommunities.htm, accessed 26th June 2012

Moore, M (2001) Political Underdevelopment: What causes 'bad governance', **Public Management Review**, Vol 3(3)

Nepal Rastra Bank (2012) **Publications: Economic Reports** [online] http://red.nrb.org.np/publica.php?tp=economic_reports&&vw=15, accessed 30th June 2012

Niebel, D (2011) **Mutual Benefits: Migration, Development, and the Economy: a necessary re-evaluation**, German Council of Foreign Relations (DGAP)

NRN UK [online], **Non-Resident Nepali United Kingdom**, http://www.nrnuk.org/, accessed 29th June 2012

Page, B and Mercer, C (2012) Why do people do stuff? Reconceptualising remittance behaviour in Diaspora-development research and policy, **Progress in Development Studies**, Vol 12(1)

Public Interest Research Centre (2011) **The Common Cause Handbook**, PIRC, Wales

Ratha, D (2011), **Whatever happened to Nepal's Diaspora bonds?** [online] http://blogs.worldbank.org/peoplemove/whatever-happened-to-nepals-diaspora-bonds, accessed 24th January 2012

Ratha, D (Ongoing) **People Move: a blog about migration, remittance and development** [online] http://blogs.worldbank.org/peoplemove/, accessed 13th June 2012, World Bank

Ratha, D, Mohapatra, S and Scheja, E (2011) Impact of Migration on Economic and Social Development, **World Bank Policy Research Working Paper 5558**

Ratha, D and Plaza, S (2011) Harnessing Diasporas, **Finance & Development**, IMF, Vol 48 (3)

Sachs, J (2005) **The End of Poverty: Economic Possibilities for Our Time**, Penguin, New York

Sapkota, C (2012) Un-feathered Cap, **Republica**, Nepal Republic Media Pvt. Ltd, Kathmandu

Shrestha, S (2010) **Effect of Educational Returns Abroad on Domestic Schooling**, Unpublished paper, University of Michigan

Singer, P (2009) **The Life You Can Save: Acting Now To End World Poverty**, Picador, New York

Taggart, F (2011) **Nepal capital tops quake risk list**, AFP News Service

(The) Telegraph, 21st February 2011, **The Gurkhas in Aldershot: Little Nepal**

UK Border Agency, **Settlement for Gurkhas** [online] http://www.ukba.homeoffice.gov.uk/visas-immigration/settlement/applicationtypes/gurkhas/ Accessed 16th January 2012

UNDP, **Human Development Reports 2011** [online] http://hdr.undp.org/en/statistics/, accessed 18th April 2012

World Bank (2011) **Migration And Remittances Factbook 2011**, 2nd Edition, World Bank, Washington

World Bank (2012) **Data for Nepal** [online] http://data.worldbank.org/country/nepal, accessed 27th June 2012

World Bank South Asia (2011) **Summary of Discussion: Consultation on South Asian Research, Education and Innovation** [online] http://go.worldbank.org/02XZDCV3S0, accessed 9th July 2012

Wroe, M and Doney, M (2010) All to play for..., **Developments: One World a Million Stories**, DfID